# Contents

Some words are shown in bold, **like this**. You can find out what they mean by looking in the glossary.

# What is a mushroom?

This mass of mushrooms is growing at the bottom of an old tree.

A mushroom is a kind of **fungus**. A fungus is like a plant but it has no green leaves.

Spore

Growing underground

Button mushrooms

# LIFE CYCLE OF A...

# Mushroom

### Revised and Updated

## Angela Royston

Heinemann
LIBRARY

**www.heinemannlibrary.co.uk**
Visit our website to find out more information about Heinemann Library books.

**To order:**
 Phone +44 (0) 1865 888066
Fax +44 (0) 1865 314091
Visit www.heinemannlibrary.co.uk

Edited by Adrian Vigliano, Harriet Milles, Diyan Leake
Designed by Kimberly R. Miracle and Tony Miracle
Original illustrations © Capstone Global Library Limited 1998, 2009
Illustrated by Alan Fraser
Picture research by Tracy Cummins
Originated by Chroma Graphics (Overseas) Pte Ltd
Printed in China by South China Printing Company Ltd

ISBN 978 0 431 99958 6 (hardback)
13 12 11 10 09
10 9 8 7 6 5 4 3 2 1

ISBN 978 0 431 99940 1 (hardback)
13 12 11 10 09
10 9 8 7 6 5 4 3 2 1

**British Library Cataloguing in Publication Data**
Royston, Angela.
  Life cycle of a mushroom. -- 2nd ed.
  1. Mushrooms--Life cycles--Juvenile literature.
  I. Title II. Mushroom
  579.6-dc22

**Acknowledgements**
We would like to thank the following for permission to reproduce photographs: Alamy pp. 24 (© Natural Visions), 29 right (© Natural Visions); Ardea p. 21 (© D.W. Greenslade); Photolibrary pp. 9 (© OSF/Barrie Watts), 10 (© OSF/G.I. Bernard), 16 (© Sue Darlow), 19 (© David M. Dennis), 22 (© Michael Diggin), 27 (© OSF/G.I. Bernard); Photoshot pp. 8 (© NHPA/Stephen Dalton), 12 (© Bruce Coleman/Hans Reinhard), 26 (© NHPA/G.I. Bernard), 28 top right (© NHPA/Stephen Dalton), 28 bottom (© Bruce Coleman/Hans Reinhard); Shutterstock pp. 4, 5 (© Yufeng Wang), 6 (© Steve Smith Photography), 7 (© Paul Atkinson), 11 (© Nicholas Rjabow), 13 (© Kathy Piper), 14 (© Peter Barrett), 15 (© Magdalena Bujak), 17 (© V Krv), 18 (© Marie Cloke), 20 (© WebStudio24h), 23 (© Arkadiy Yarmolenko), 25 (© T-Design), 28 top left (© Steve Smith Photography), 29 left (© Marie Cloke).

Cover photograph reproduced with permission of Alamy (© imagebroker).

We would like to thank Michael Bright for his invaluable help in the preparation of this book.

Every effort has been made to contact copyright holders of material reproduced in this book. Any omissions will be rectified in subsequent printings if notice is given to the publisher.

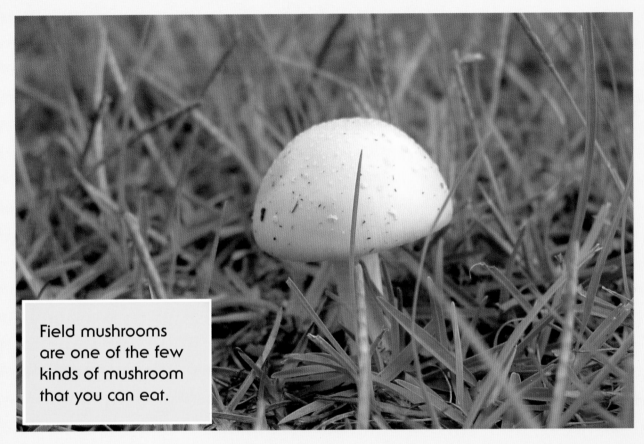

Field mushrooms are one of the few kinds of mushroom that you can eat.

There are thousands of different kinds of fungi. This book is about a field mushroom.

Growing in the field

Ripe mushrooms

5 years

# A small beginning

This picture shows the underside of a mushroom.

Like all kinds of **fungi**, mushrooms begin life as tiny **spores** in autumn. The spores grow on the underside of the parent mushroom.

Spore

Growing underground

Button mushrooms

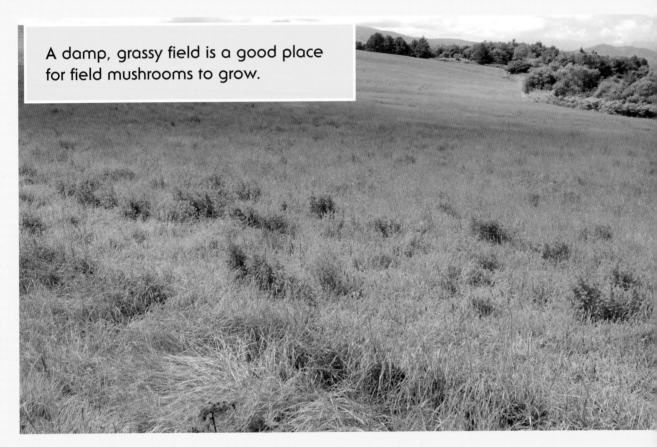

A damp, grassy field is a good place for field mushrooms to grow.

Millions of spores blow away from the parent mushroom. Some of the spores land on moist **soil**.

Growing in the field

Ripe mushrooms

5 years

# Growing underground

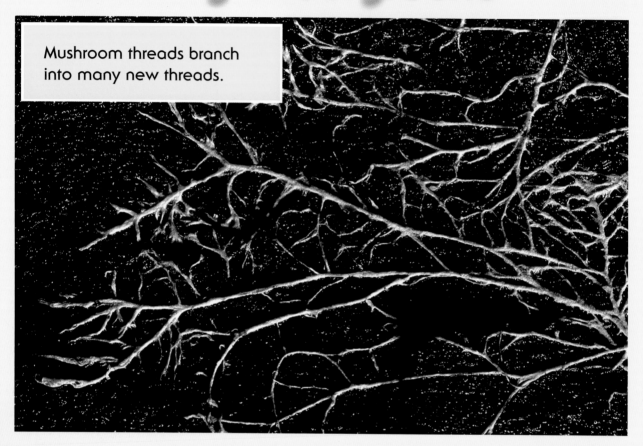

Mushroom threads branch into many new threads.

A tiny **thread** grows out from the **spore**. The thread grows longer and longer.

Spore

Growing underground

Button mushrooms

Mushroom threads can cover a wide area underground.

The threads take in food and water from the **soil**. Some threads join together with threads from other spores.

Growing in the field

Ripe mushrooms

5 years

# The next 12 months

Warm, damp soil helps the mushroom grow.

In late summer, the **soil** is warm and damp. A small mushroom begins to grow underground on part of the web of **threads**.

Spore

Growing underground

Button mushrooms

Other mushrooms are growing too. They live on the food and water taken in by the threads.

The mushrooms look like buttons when they are small.

# Growing in the field

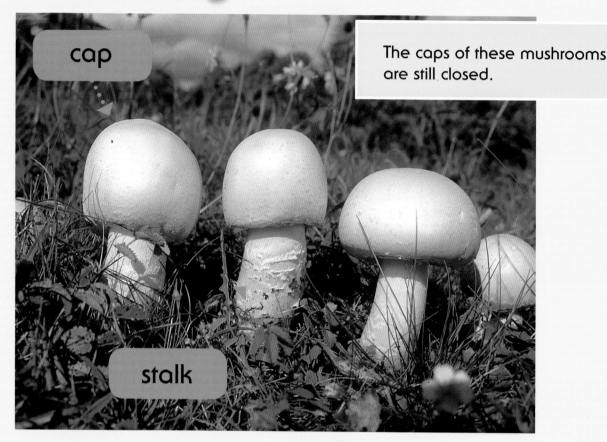

cap

The caps of these mushrooms are still closed.

stalk

As the mushrooms grow bigger, the **stalks** push up through the **soil**. The top of the mushroom is called the cap.

Spore

Growing underground

Button mushrooms

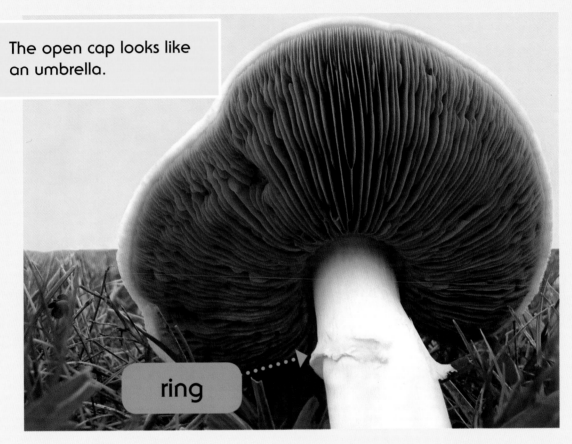

The open cap looks like an umbrella.

ring

The mushroom cap opens up. There is a ring of thin skin where the cap was joined to the stalk.

Growing in the field

Ripe mushrooms

5 years

# Food for animals

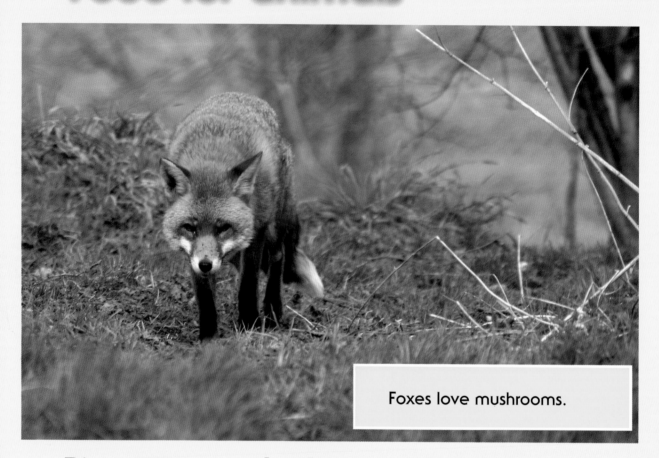

Foxes love mushrooms.

Pigs, mice, and other animals eat some of the mushrooms.

Spore

Growing underground

Button mushrooms

A fox can smell mushrooms in a field.

When a fox smells the mushrooms, it picks one or two and chews them up.

Growing in the field

Ripe mushrooms

5 years

# Next day

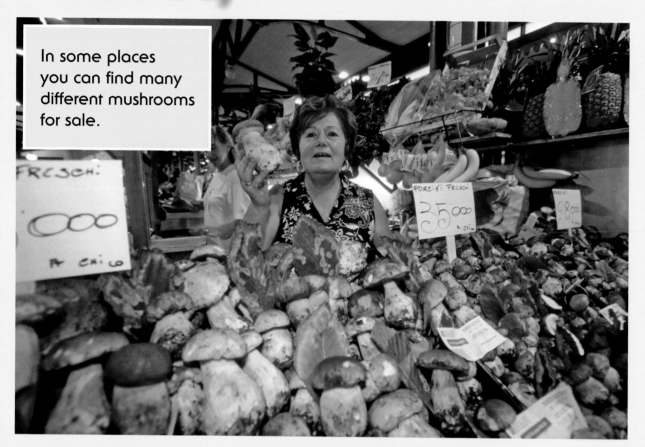

In some places you can find many different mushrooms for sale.

People like to eat mushrooms too. You can buy mushrooms in a supermarket or on a market stall.

Spore

Growing underground

Button mushrooms

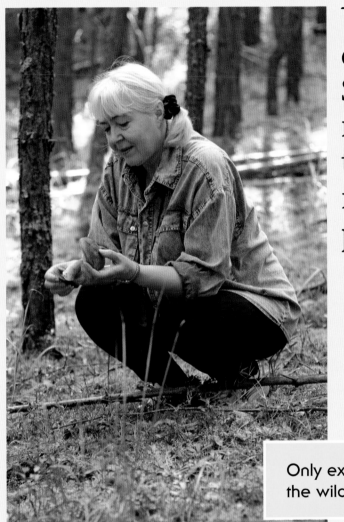

This woman is a mushroom **expert**. She knows which mushrooms are safe to pick. Some **wild** mushrooms are **poisonous**.

Only experts should pick mushrooms in the wild.

Growing in the field

Ripe mushrooms

5 years

# New spores

The spores of the field mushroom give the gills their brown colour.

gills

The underside of the mushroom cap is covered with thin ridges called **gills**. The gills are covered with millions of **spores**.

Spore

Growing underground

Button mushrooms

This picture is a close-up of gill cells (blue) and spores (purple-brown spots).

The tiny building blocks of living things are called cells. Spores are made inside special cells along a mushroom's gills.

Growing in the field

Ripe mushrooms

5 years

# 1 day later

After the spores are carried away in the wind, the mushroom dies.

Sometimes the wind can blow **spores** a long way. Some spores from the field mushroom ended up in the forest.

Spore

Growing underground

Button mushrooms

Many kinds of **fungi** grow in the forest. But the **soil** in the forest is not right for the field mushroom. Its spores will not grow there.

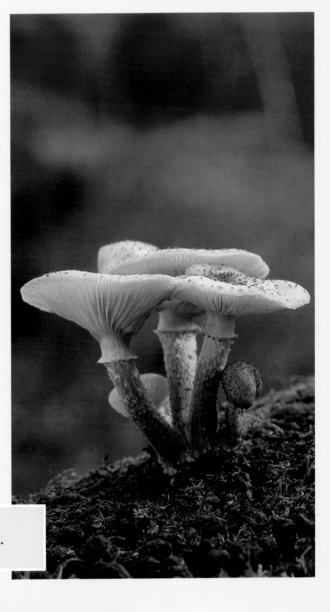

This honey fungus grows in the forest.

Growing in the field

Ripe mushrooms

5 years

# 1 year later

Some field mushroom **spores** fell in this meadow. They grew and made new mushrooms.

Field mushrooms grow in wet grasslands.

Spore

Growing underground

Button mushrooms

The threads in the old field made new mushrooms too.

In late summer the new mushrooms pushed up through the ground.

Growing in the field

Ripe mushrooms

5 years

# 5 years later

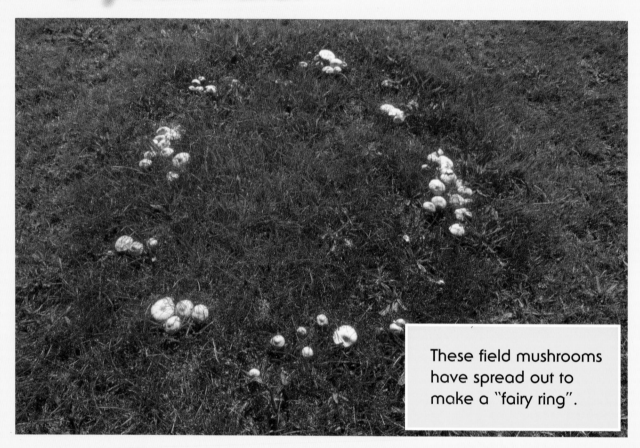

These field mushrooms have spread out to make a "fairy ring".

Every year the underground **threads** grow to make new mushrooms.

Spore

Growing underground

Button mushrooms

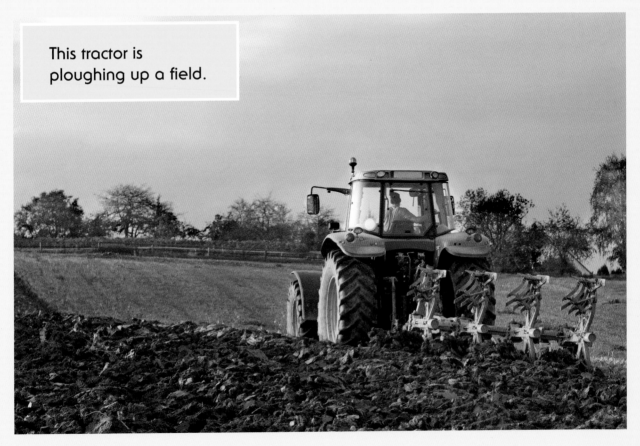

This tractor is ploughing up a field.

When a tractor breaks up the **soil** and turns it over, the threads of all the **fungi** are broken too.

Growing in the field

Ripe mushrooms

5 years

# A mushroom farm

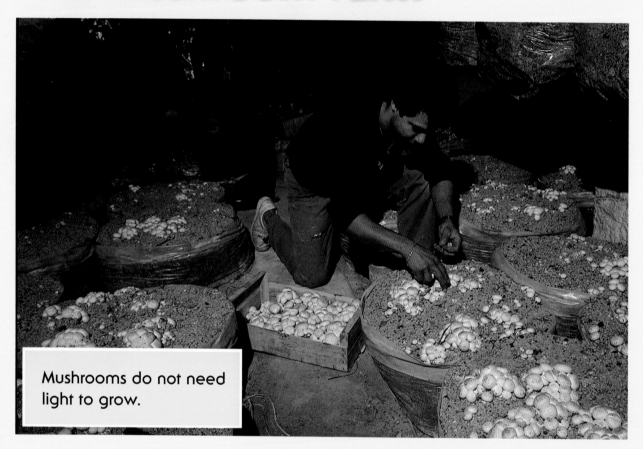

Mushrooms do not need light to grow.

Most of the mushrooms we eat are grown on special mushroom farms.

Spore

Growing underground

Button mushrooms

These mushrooms are growing in underground caves.

New mushrooms can grow all the time in damp places.

Growing in the field

Ripe mushrooms

5 years

# Life cycle

Spores

Growing underground

Button mushrooms

Ripe mushrooms

5 years later

# Fact file

- There are about 3,300 different kinds of mushroom.

- Each mushroom produces up to 40 million **spores** every hour for about two days. Only a few of these will grow into new mushrooms.

- A few kinds of mushrooms are so **poisonous** they can kill you if you eat them, so do not pick **wild** mushrooms.

- Long ago, people used to think that "fairy rings" were made by fairies dancing and that the mushrooms were seats the fairies sat on to rest.

# Glossary

**expert**    someone who knows a lot about something

**fungus** (**fungi** for more than one)   a living thing that is like a plant but which cannot make food for itself the way that green plants can

**gills**    the soft brown underside of a mushroom cap

**poisonous**    able to cause illness or death if eaten

**soil**    the layer of mud that covers much of the land

**spore**    part of a mushroom that can grow into new fungi

**stalk**    stem that joins the cap of a mushroom to its underground threads

**thread**    fine strand, like a hair

**wild**    growing or living without the help of people

# More books to read

*How do Plants and Animals Change?* (Looking at Life Cycles), Angela Royston (Enslow Elementary, 2008)

*How do Plants Grow?* (World of Plants), Louise and Richard Spilsbury (Heinemann Library, 2006)

*Plant Life Cycle* (Macmillan Library: Earth's Cycles), Cheryl Jakab (Nelson Thornes, 2008)

# Index